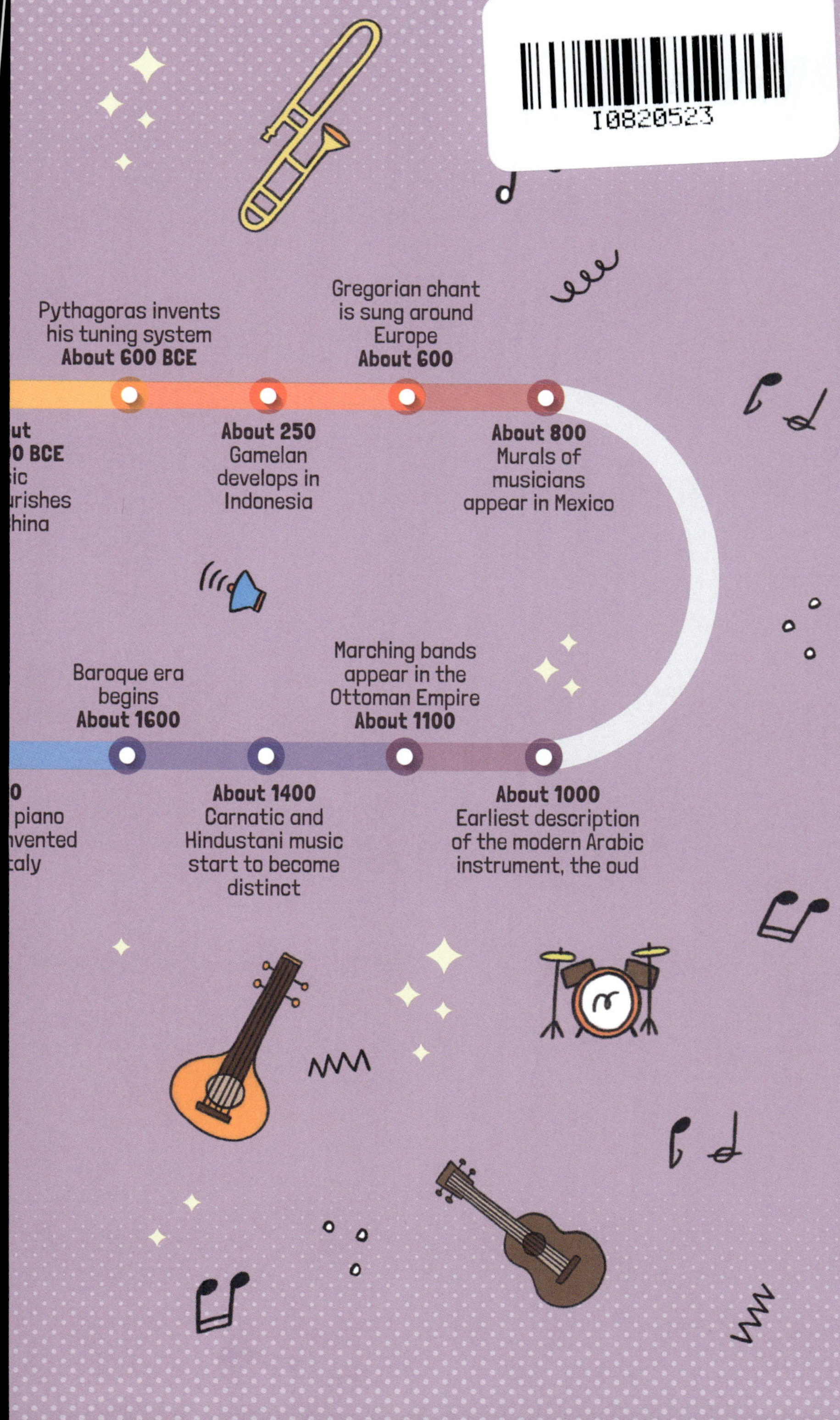
I0820523
Pythagoras invents his tuning system
About 600 BCE
Gregorian chant is sung around Europe
About 600
About 250
Gamelan develops in Indonesia
About 800
Murals of musicians appear in Mexico
Baroque era begins
About 1600
Marching bands appear in the Ottoman Empire
About 1100
About 1400
Carnatic and Hindustani music start to become distinct
About 1000
Earliest description of the modern Arabic instrument, the oud

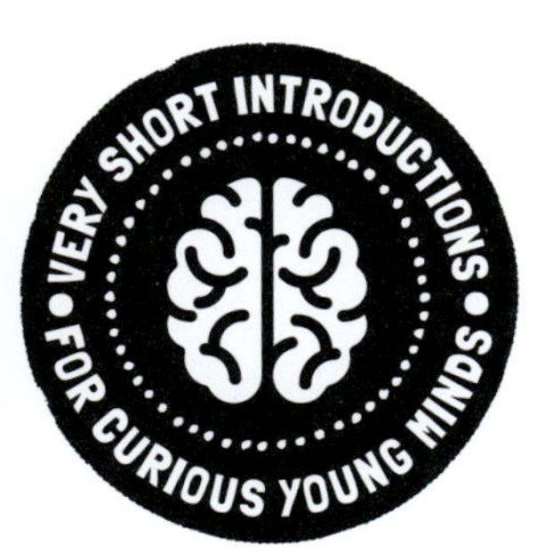

The WORLD of MUSIC

Professor Nathan Holder

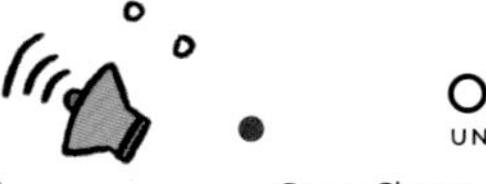

Great Clarendon Street, Oxford OX2 6DP

Oxford University Press is a department of the University of Oxford. It furthers the University's objective of excellence in research, scholarship, and education by publishing worldwide. Oxford is a registered trade mark of Oxford University Press in the UK and in certain other countries

Text written by Professor Nathan Holder
Illustrated by Octavia Bromell, Ana Seixas, and Crissie Rodda

Designed and edited by Raspberry Books Ltd

First published 2024
This hardback edition published 2026

Library of Congress Cataloging-in-Publication

Data is available

ISBN 978-1-382-07230-4

1 3 5 7 9 10 8 6 4 2

The manufacturing process conforms to the environmental regulations of the country of origin.

Printed in China

The manufacturer's authorised representative in the EU for product safety is Oxford University Press España S.A. of El Parque Empresarial San Fernando de Henares, Avenida de Castilla, 2 – 28830 Madrid (www.oup.es/en or product.safety@oup.com). OUP España S.A. also acts as importer into Spain of products made by the manufacturer.

Acknowledgments

The publisher and authors would like to thank the following for permission to use photographs and other copyright material:

Cover artwork: Crissie Rodda, Octavia Bromell, and Ana Seixas. **Cover photo:** Pavlo S/Shutterstock. **Inside Photos:** p1(tl): Pavlo S/Shutterstock; p9: Tricon Infotech/Shutterstock; p12(a): Arcady/Shutterstock; p12(b): Ilya Arkinshin/Shutterstock; p12(c): Egor Shilov/Shutterstock; p12(d): Mary Erskine/Shutterstock; p12(e): Starstov/Shutterstock; p12(f): newelle/Shutterstock; p12(g): NadzeyaShanchuk/Shutterstock; p12(h): In art/Shutterstock; p18: Album / Alamy Stock Photo; p19: Copyright © 2023 Apple Inc. All rights reserved; p28: Molotok289/Shutterstock; p31: Morphart creation/Shutterstock; p35(l): Alemon cz/Shutterstock; p35(r): Arc Tina/Shutterstock; p39: Mountainpix/Shutterstock; p41: ruzanna/Shutterstock; p42: Mindscape studio/Shutterstock; p43: Dzha33/Shutterstock; p44: Daniel Jarosch/Shutterstock; p48: i3D/Shutterstock; p53: Peter Hermes Furian/Shutterstock; p57: Krugloff/Shutterstock; p64: photostar 72/Shutterstock; p65: Nicku/Shutterstock; p68: Shumer/Shutterstock; p73: Kariakin Aleksandr/Shutterstock; pp84-85: Dervish45/Shutterstock; p87: Richard Griffin/Shutterstock. **Front end paper:** pp2-3: Aleksandr Bryliaev/Shutterstock. **Back end paper:** p2: Pavlo S/Shutterstock.

Author photo courtesy of Benjamin Ealovega.

Artwork by **Octavia Bromell**, **Ana Seixas**, Crissie Rodda, Ekaterina Gorelova, Adam Quest, Geraldine Sy, Aaron Cushley, Raspberry Books, and Oxford University Press.

Every effort has been made to contact copyright holders of material reproduced in this book. Any omissions will be rectified in subsequent printings if notice is given to the publisher.

Contents

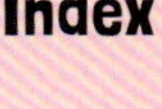

Chapter 1

What is Music?

It has been said that no culture or civilization on Earth has ever existed without music. Without a time machine it's really hard to prove, but it's not that hard to believe.

Music is in everything we do. It can make us laugh, cry, feel energized, or even help us learn (try saying your ABCs without singing them!). Many people might sing while they cook, or play music to keep them company on long journeys. Music has been played, written about, and experienced in many different ways, by many different cultures and people across time.

So what is music? It's hard to define, but here's one way to think about it—music is collections of sounds that can help us to express our emotions and connect with people.

It's also a powerful form of communication—music created hundreds of years ago can still make us emotional, and can help us to understand various cultures, experiences, ideas, and how people thought and felt. Music and lyrics of the past can help us to understand what life was like hundreds of years ago—almost like a time machine!

Music can also be deeply spiritual. In ancient times, philosophers in China and Greece wrote about how the right music could help people be kind and respectful citizens. Music is used in religion—for example, it often plays a crucial part in Christian worship services, where singing songs helps people to connect with God, and with each other.

Music is so powerful that it can bring back happy memories of friends and relatives who have died, or special times in our lives. Because of this, music has been used as a form of therapy since the nineteenth century and this has become more common recently as music therapists have explored how music can help people facing challenges with their mental health or processing trauma.

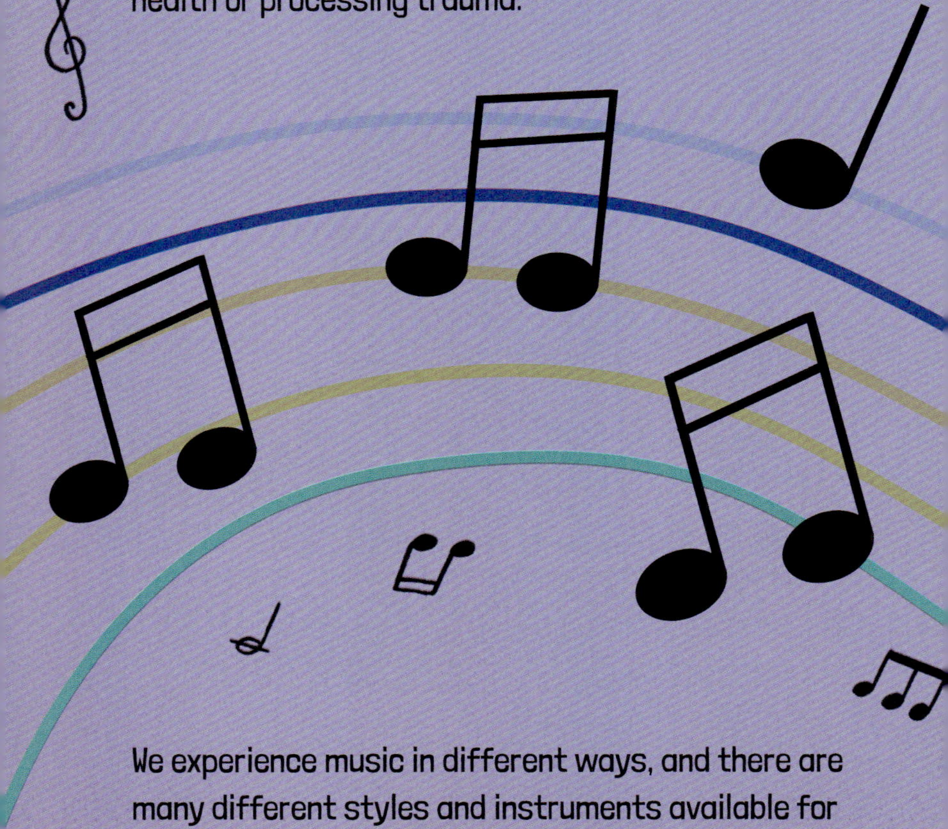

We experience music in different ways, and there are many different styles and instruments available for us to listen to, play, and enjoy. This is great, but it also means that there is so much music out there, we won't be able to cover everything in this book!

As we dive into the world of music, we will explore different musical styles, instruments, and incredible musicians. From advertising to mental health, education to entertainment, music has been an **instrumental** part of human existence for thousands of years.

In this very short introduction to music, you'll discover that . . .

We've been playing flutes for over **40,000 years**.

Music has played a vital part in **protests**.

Music **connects** us with each other.

Slow music makes you shop for longer.

Your **voice** is a musical instrument.

Read on to discover more about the **wonderful world of music . . .**

Chapter 2

Music and Science

Have you ever noticed how the sound of a washing machine changes the faster it spins? Have you ever felt the bass from a loudspeaker pump through your body? Science can help us understand how music works and how it affects us all.

Good vibrations

Sounds are simply vibrations! The individual atoms that we and everything around us are made of are constantly vibrating at different speeds. These vibrations are so small that we never hear or see them. However, when larger objects, like our **vocal cords** or wooden rattles, vibrate very quickly, we experience these vibrations as sound.

In between the ears

Many people develop the ability to hear very early, even before they are born. When we hear music, we are listening to lots of different vibrations at the same time, which travel in sound waves into our ears and then into our brains where we make sense of what we are hearing.

Inside our ears, our eardrums vibrate and send signals to three small bones called the incus, malleus, and stapes, which **amplify** the sound. These signals travel to the cochlea, which is a snail-shaped bone that contains fluid. Tiny hairs respond to waves caused by that fluid, which in turn send electric signals to the auditory nerve. All this happens in less than 0.05 seconds. **Wow!**

Through evolution and social conditioning, humans have learned to recognize certain sounds and categorize them as loud, high, quiet, sharp, etc.

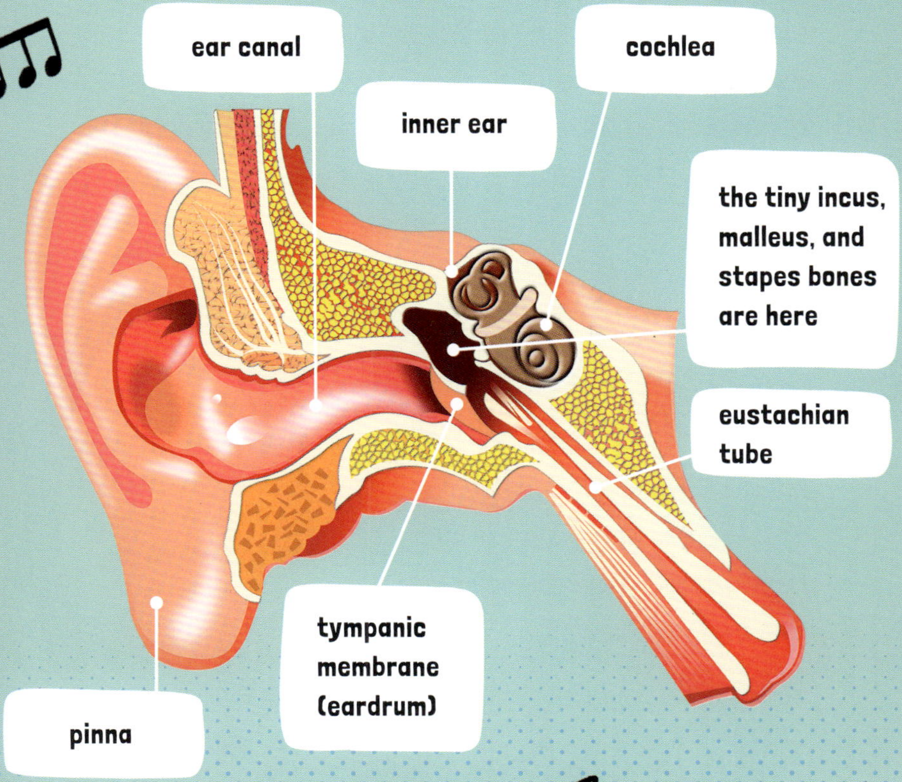

Not everyone hears sounds in the same way. Musicians such as Ludwig van Beethoven have shown us that, however you experience sound, you can create amazing music.

Beethoven was a **composer** from Germany who was born in 1770. He composed many pieces of music throughout his life, but he composed one of his most famous, **Symphony** No. 9, in 1824 when he had **significant hearing loss.**

Dame Evelyn Glennie is a famous Scottish solo **percussionist** who started losing her hearing at age eight. She plays many different instruments, such as gongs and bells, and often plays barefoot as she chooses to experience the music on stage through the vibrations her instruments make.

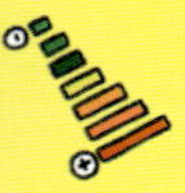

MUSIC HERO

DAME EVELYN GLENNIE

Musician, composer, and public speaker. She has won over 100 international awards, including two Grammy Awards.

Frequency and pitch

Frequency is the number of vibrations or cycles an object makes in a specific period of time. The result of these vibrations is sound, which travels in waves. The higher the frequency (shorter wavelengths) the higher the pitch of the sound will be. The lower the frequency, the lower the pitch.

The same thing happens with ceiling fans or helicopter propellers. The faster and more frequently they spin (short **wavelengths**), the higher and louder the sound they produce.

The slower the fan or propeller spins (long wavelengths), the quieter and lower the sound.

High frequency = high pitch

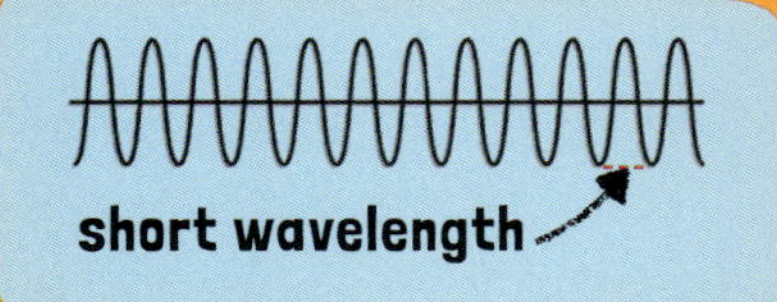

Low frequency = low pitch

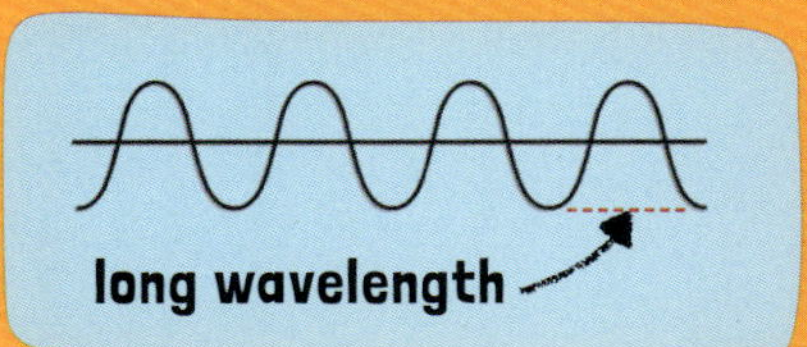

Pitch is how high or low a sound is.

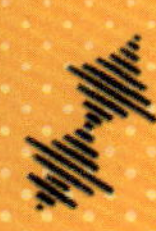

Speak like a Musician

HERTZ

Frequencies of sound are measured in hertz (Hz), a unit named after German scientist Heinrich Hertz.

Humans can't hear all the frequencies in the world. If we could, it would probably be too much to handle!

The common range of hearing in humans is 20 Hz to 20,000 Hz, with 20 Hz being the lowest sound and 20,000 Hz the highest. Our hearing changes over time and many people find it harder to hear higher frequency sounds. Other animals can hear different ranges to us, which explains why we can't hear the high frequencies produced by dog whistles, for example.

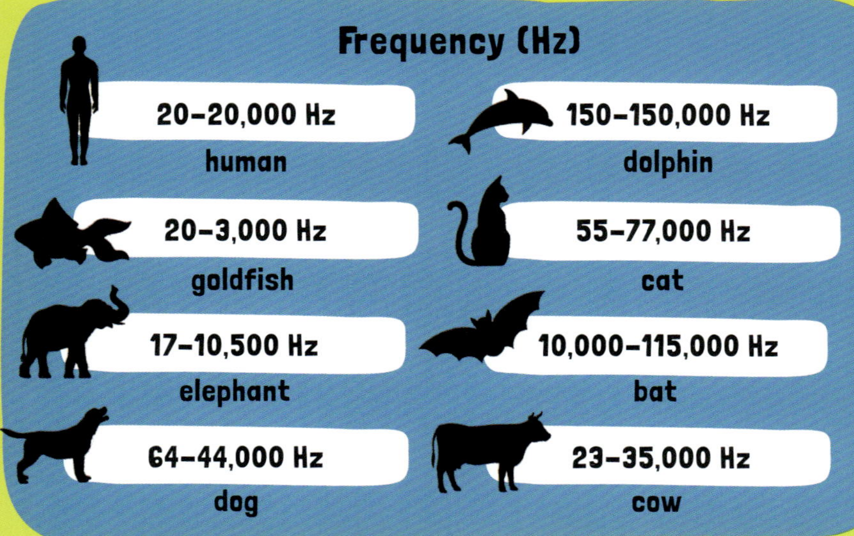

At around 20 Hz, the sounds humans hear are low and pulsating. As the wavelengths get shorter and sounds are heard in the 30 Hz to 55 Hz range, many people can start to recognize individual notes. The lowest note on a standard eighty-eight key piano is 27.5 Hz, and a large didgeridoo can play a low note at around 55 Hz. As a general rule, the **bigger** the instrument, the **lower** the frequency it can produce.

Frequency (Hz)

- clarinet: 150–2,000 Hz
- piano: 27.5–4,000 Hz
- harp: 30–3,500 Hz
- steelpan: 55–1,500 Hz
- violin: 200–2,500 Hz
- sitar: 65–1,000 Hz
- gambang: 100–2,000 Hz
- didgeridoo: 55–80 Hz

So if that's how people physically hear, how did we start to organize these sounds?

Tuning

To figure out a way to order these frequencies, people began to develop "**tuning** systems" to make it easier to create music and play together.

It is said that around 2,500 years ago, the Greek philosopher Pythagoras helped to further develop a tuning system from **Mesopotamia**. He explored sounds by plucking a piece of string and making it vibrate. He soon realized that halving the piece of string made it vibrate twice as fast, and it produced a note that sounded the same but was higher in pitch. This was called an **octave**. Pythagoras realized that by continuing to halve the piece of string, he was able to create a **scale** with eight notes.

In the **Western European classical** tradition, these notes were named A, B, C, D, E, F, and G, where each letter name is a specific frequency (A is 440 Hz, C is 523.25 Hz) and helped to popularize a tuning system.

Pythagoras's system was used for hundreds of years in Western Europe until other systems took over.

Another system, called **equal temperament**, was first written about in the sixteenth century by Zhu Zaiyu.

Speak like a Musician

EQUAL TEMPERAMENT

Equal temperament is the system that divides an octave into twelve equal parts (12 Tone Equal Temperament or 12-TET for short). This system forms the basis of a lot of Western European and North American popular music.

MUSIC HERO

ZHU ZAIYU

Chinese musician, scientist, mathematician, and prince who wrote about a system of musical tuning called equal temperament.

One octave on a keyboard divided into 12-TET looks like this—it might look familiar to you.

This isn't the only way that people divide up a scale. There are notes in between called semitones or quarter tones. An Arabic system uses these tones to divide an octave into twenty-four equal notes (24-TET). Other systems use thirty-one or even seventy-two notes. Instruments like the **oud** and the **qanun** allow musicians to play semi and quarter tones much more easily than, for example, pianos.

Volume

That takes care of the range humans can hear, but what about the volume? Sound is measured in **decibels** (dB).

Being around music consistently played at very high volumes can permanently damage hearing and cause pain, so it's important to protect the ears. Some of the loudest concerts ever recorded have reached over 130 dB. In 2009, in a concert in Ottowa, Canada, the **rock** band Kiss reached 136 dB—ouch!

So there you have it. A whistle-stop tour (get it? Whistle??) of some of the science behind music. But which words and phrases do musicians use to talk about all of these waves and frequencies? **The next chapter will reveal all . . .**

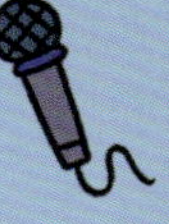

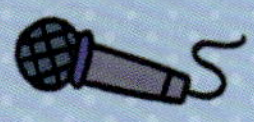

Music Theory

Music theory is how some musicians try to explain the music they hear, or the notation they see.

Music theory gives us words and symbols that allow us to compare, find patterns, and discover how musicians have made music to create certain feelings or share ideas. It also gives us rules that can help us to create our own music.

Music notation

Music notation is any system of symbols that helps us write down the sounds we hear, or want to hear. It also can give people the instructions they need to play the music, and helps us to document and pass music down through generations.

The oldest music notation found is over 4,000 years old and comes from ancient Mesopotamia. The oldest song ever found was written over 3,500 years ago, again in Mesopotamia, and is called the Hurrian Hymn No. 6.

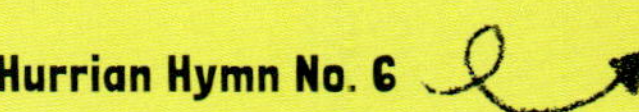
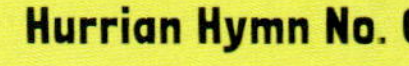

Hurrian Hymn No. 6

Graphic **scores** use shapes, colors, symbols, and art to represent the sounds that someone has heard, or wants to hear. Composers can also use graphic scores to give performers directions and instructions that are difficult to describe! These can be very personal—sometimes a composer will have to explain what the squiggles, colors, and patterns mean. Other composers may not give many instructions but will allow performers to interpret the score as they feel.

Digital Audio Workstations (DAWs) are computer programs that allow people to create music electronically. Some have features that represent sounds with lines and colors to show how loud (darker colors) or soft (lighter colors) a note is.

Digital Audio Workstation (DAW)

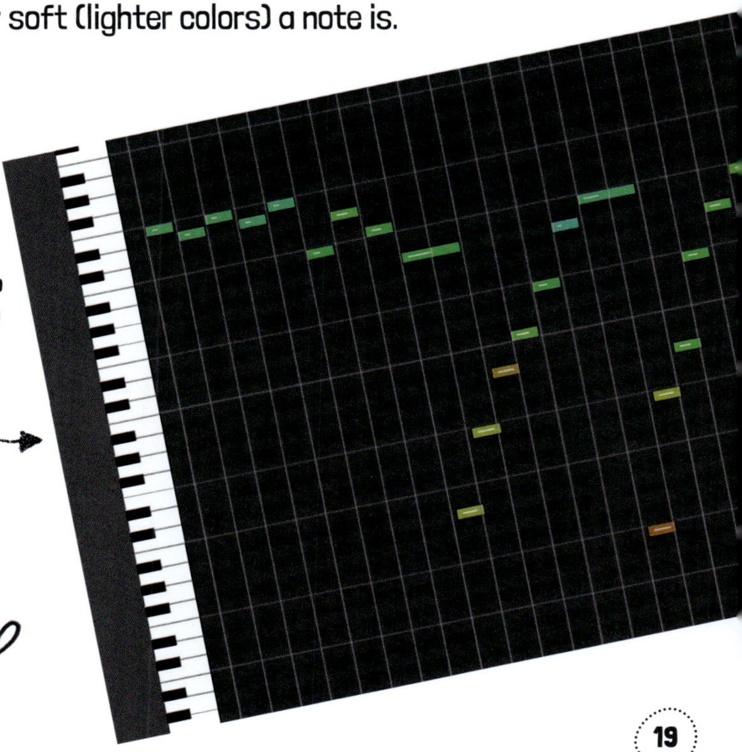

Often, when people use the phrase "music theory" they're only talking about a Western European way of understanding music, which evolved in the seventeenth and eighteenth centuries. These ideas spread during the time of **colonization**, when ways of understanding and playing music from outside of Europe were destroyed or banned, because many Europeans thought they were inferior. But theories of music were developing long before then . . .

Some of the earliest music theories came from Mesopotamia around 1500 BCE, China around 250 BCE, and India around 200 BCE. As musicians learned from each other, and technology and sciences evolved, these theories evolved as well. While there are different ways of thinking about music, there are certain things many musical styles have in common.

We'll find out what these words mean **as we go on.**

Feel the rhythm

Many theories around the world recognize that sounds can be ordered into beats of different lengths. In Western European theory, **rhythms** are notated like this:

- **semibreve = 4 beats**
- **minim = 2 beats**
- **crotchet = 1 beat**
- **quaver = half beat**
- **semiquaver = quarter beat**

By joining these individual notes together, we can create recognizable rhythms. An easy way to remember certain rhythms is to set them to words like these:

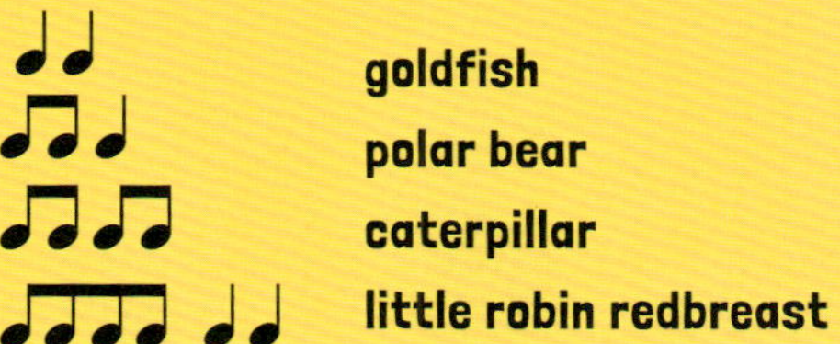

Rhythms can be described as fast, slow, or even **"bouncy"** or "complex."

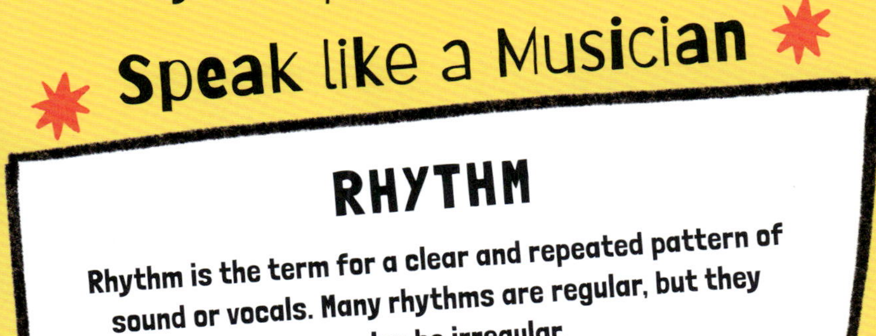

In **Indian classical** music, rhythm is called taal or tala, which tells us how many beats are to be counted. If there are twelve beats, when we arrive at twelve we start the cycle again.

Taal is more about how the music is structured rather than groups of individual notes. There are many different taal including:

Teen taal: 16 beats
Ek taal: 12 beats
Jhap taal: 10 beats
Matta taal: 9 beats
Keharwa taal: 8 beats
Rupak taal: 7 beats
Dadra taal: 6 beats

Time signatures

A time signature shows how many beats are in one cycle, or bar. They are usually written as two numbers—the top one tells us the number of beats and the bottom one tell us what kind of beat it is.

6/8 time signature

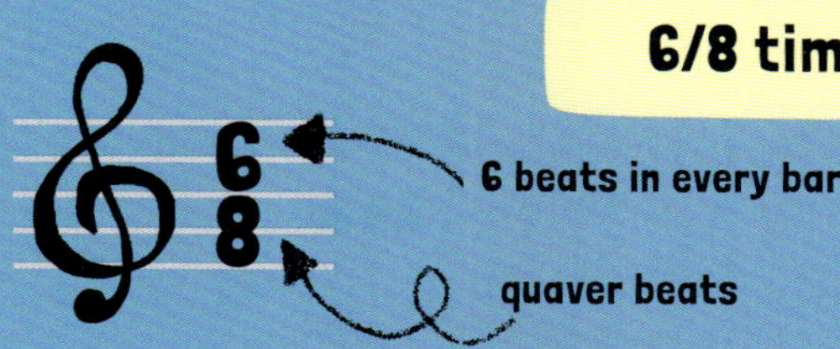

Speak like a Musician

TREBLE CLEF

The treble clef is a symbol used in Western European music theory that helps musicians to identify notes.

People have written music in many different time signatures, and some switch between different time signatures in the same piece. In 1959, the **jazz** pianist Dave Brubeck released an album called *Time Out*. It became an influential jazz album, partly because it explored different time signatures in a way that had been uncommon in jazz. The tune "Take Five" is in 5/4, and "Blue Rondo à la Turk" is in 9/4.

There are so many different ways of counting in **music around the world!**

Syncopation

Try saying syncopation, and put more emphasis on the **bold** letters in the black boxes:

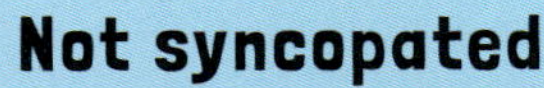

Syn- co- **pa-** tion **is** so **cool**

Syncopated

Syn- **co-** pa- **tion** is **so** cool

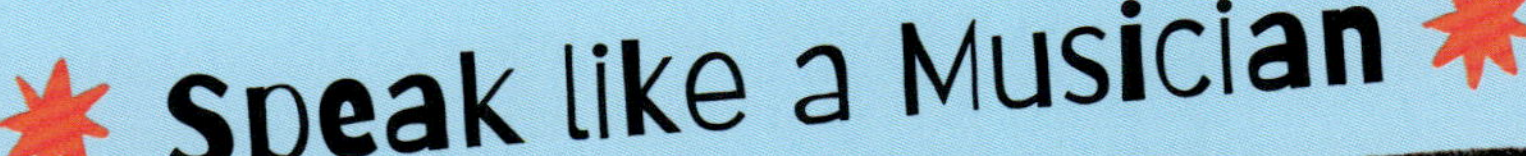

SYNCOPATION

Syncopation involves playing or stressing the weak or offbeats in a piece of music.

Scales

Scales are sets of notes arranged in a particular order. There are many different types of scales, made up of different numbers of notes. There are four-note scales (tetratonic), five-note scales (pentatonic), six-note scales (hexatonic), and so on.

In traditional Arabic music, scales are called **maqām**. Here is an example of a common maqām called Maqām Hijaz Kurd:

Here is an example of a scale using Western European notation:

A lot of traditional music from around the world was created using pentatonic (five note) scales, and many pop songs written in the last forty years use them too.

Learning how different scales work can be really important, especially for people who **improvise**. Jazz music is built around the idea of improvising, and over the years musicians have explored all sorts of ways to use scales.

Musicians who play styles like jazz and **Hindustani music** have to study different scales or **rāgas** for many years to be able to improvise well. John Coltrane was a jazz saxophonist who played on the best-selling jazz record of all time, *Kind of Blue* (1959), and was one of the most influential musicians of the twentieth century. He was obsessed with practicing scales and **arpeggios** for up to ten hours a day!

John Coltrane

A composer's toolkit

We're used to listening to music that uses all of these elements at the same time, and composers sometimes spend a lot of time deciding how to use them all. They have to decide the speed of a song (**tempo**), which instruments to use (**timbre**), how many instruments are playing at the same time (**texture**), what the **melody** of the song will be, what **chords** they want to use (harmony), and many other things!

Speak like a Musician

CHORDS

Chords are three or more notes played at the same time.

ARPEGGIO

In an arpeggio, the notes of a chord are played separately in ascending or descending order.

TEMPO

Tempo is a technical word for how fast or slow music is and is usually measured in beats per minute (bpm), so 60 bpm means one beat a second.

In Western European music theory, Italian words are often used for specific tempos. Some of these include:

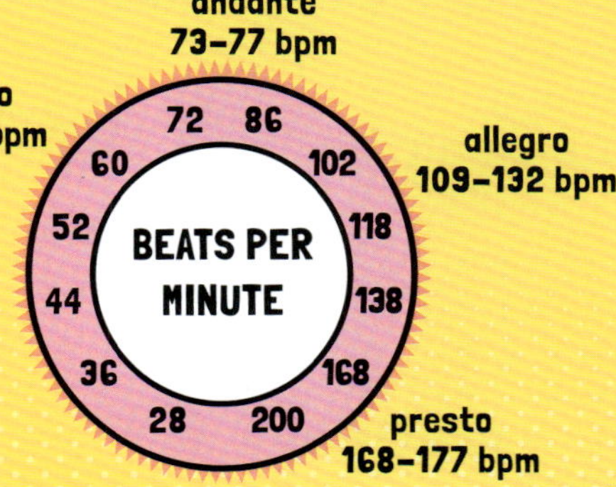

Using different tempos in one song is very common in many styles of music, including **klezmer** and metal. Sometimes these changes in tempo are gradual, or they can be very sudden.

Another element is timbre. If a steelpan and a violin played the same note, they would sound different, right? This is because the shape, size, and material an instrument is made from affects how it vibrates and the sound it produces. This is timbre—the specific vibrations and frequencies that help us to recognize instruments by their sound. An instrument could have a tinny timbre (like a triangle), or a rich timbre (like a **cello**). Choosing the right instruments that work together could be the difference between a great song and a song that not everyone would enjoy.

a violin

a triangle

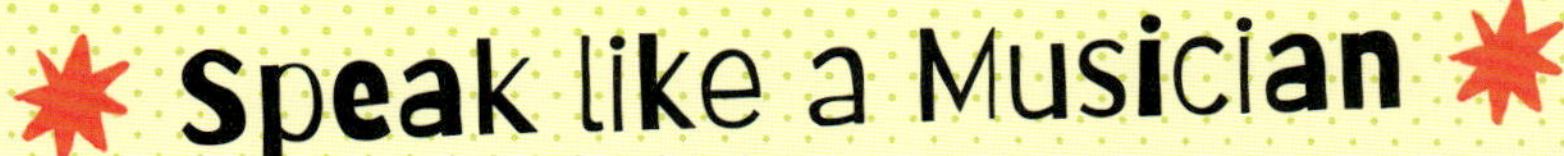

Speak like a Musician

TEXTURE

Texture describes layers of music. Lots of instruments playing at the same time is a thick texture, and a few instruments playing a few notes is a thin texture. Using different textures in the same song can make it more interesting.

MELODY

A melody is a series of notes or sounds usually forming the part of a song people remember and sing along to. Songwriters can spend a lot of time creating a melody that is new, but also catchy and easy to sing.

HARMONY

We get harmony when more than two notes are played at the same time. Harmony can also mean the chords that are played underneath a melody.

All of these elements come together to create the music you love (or dislike!). But, unless it's played live, we need a way to listen to music, don't we? Let's dive **into the world of recording . . .**

Listening and Recording

It's quite hard to imagine, but there was a time when the only way you could listen to music was if you were playing or singing, or it was being played or sung by people near you.

There was no radio, no music in the grocery store, and **silence** while you did some of your favorite activities, like washing the dishes.

Hundreds of years before the first **audio** recording, people made machines to play music. The Banū Mūsā brothers from Iraq created a water-powered organ in the ninth century, and after that there were mechanical instruments such as wind-up boxes that produced music by turning a handle, causing pieces of metal to strike small metal bumps. But even with these contraptions, only a few sounds could be produced.

A device called a phonautograph was invented in 1857, which could record sound but strangely could not play it back! The sounds were recorded **visually** on glass or on paper. A recording of Claude Debussy's *Au Clair de la Lune* was made in 1860, and in 2008 a group of researchers in America finally converted it for people to hear—it is the first recording of someone singing that we have to this day!

In 1877, the American inventor Thomas Edison invented the cylinder phonograph, which allowed people to hear recorded music for the first time. These were **wax cylinders** that could hold up to two minutes of music.

Thomas Edison

wax cylinders

The German American inventor Emile Berliner invented the gramophone in 1887, which allowed two minutes of music to be played on round, flat discs.

Berliner's discs became the most popular way of listening to music for the next sixty years. These evolved into the vinyl records many people still use today. There were three main disc sizes:

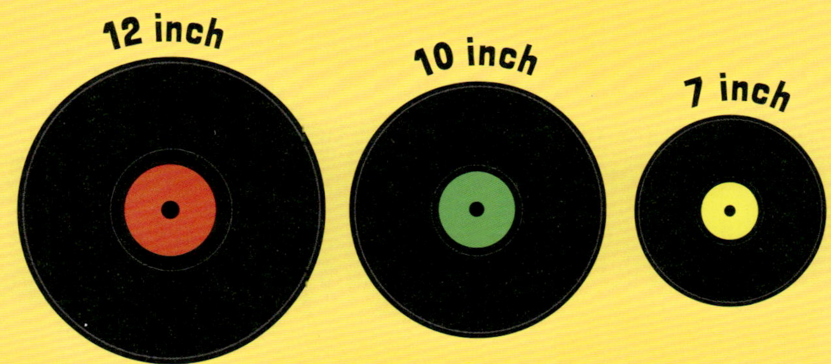

When radio was invented, music had to be played on the airwaves live, but as technology improved, records started to be broadcast worldwide.

The option to record music was a **game changer**, allowing musicians and recording companies to earn more money and have their music heard by many people around the world. This meant that recording techniques had to be developed—for example, the louder instruments had to play in the back and the quieter instruments at the front closest to the microphones so they weren't drowned out!

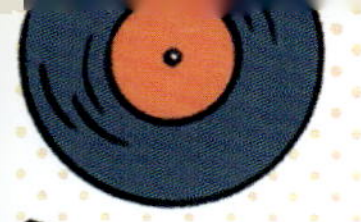

RECORDING BREAKTHROUGHS

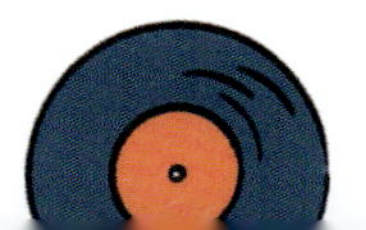

Vinyl records also allowed for new styles of music to be created. **Hip-hop** developed in New York in the 1970s when disc jockeys (DJs) like DJ Kool Herc and Grandmaster Flash played records on **turntables**. They would find the parts of **funk** records where only the drums or no vocals appeared (called the **breaks**) and play them on a loop. Dancers loved dancing during the breaks (which is where we get the term breakdance from), and it gave **emcees** (MCs) music to rap over.

In the later twentieth century, music was recorded on cassette tapes, before compact discs (CDs) became the main way to listen to music. New technologies, such as portable casette and CD players, allowed

people to listen to music wherever and whenever they wanted. You could have hours of music in your pocket. This changed people's lives, allowing them to drown out annoying noises!

The internet changed everything in the mid-1980s and beyond. Instead of recorded music only existing as a physical object, music began to be shared digitally, in formats like MP3 files. People had found ways to illegally copy music from tapes and CDs (piracy), but these new digital files allowed music to be stolen and shared illegally around the world in minutes. Musicians were not being paid for their work, and a solution was desperately needed.

At the start of the twenty-first century, streaming services became popular. These allowed users to pay for individual tracks and download them to their computers or listening devices. These days, better internet speeds mean that many people no longer need to download music at all!

All of these new technologies allowed music to spread widely, and certain musicians to become **superstars** from their record sales.

TOP-SELLING MUSCIANS FROM THE 1950s TO 2010s

1950s: ELVIS PRESLEY

127.1 MILLION RECORDS SOLD

Played early rock and roll with blues influences

1960s: THE BEATLES

376.9 MILLION RECORDS SOLD

Experimented with different styles, including skiffle, Hindustani, rock and roll, and pop

1970s: PINK FLOYD

171.7 MILLION RECORDS SOLD

Played various styles of rock music, sometimes featuring long instrumental sections

1980s: MICHAEL JACKSON

181.7 MILLION RECORDS SOLD

Played a range of very popular pop music

1990s: CELINE DION

60.1 MILLION RECORDS SOLD

Performed ballads, often with emotional themes

2000s: EMINEM

23.6 MILLION RECORDS SOLD

Played rap music with quick, witty lines and often violent themes

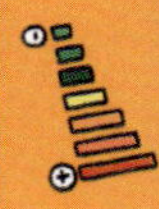

2010s: ADELE

73 MILLION RECORDS SOLD

Performed songs heavily influenced by soul music, often about relationships

Notice anything? Most of these artists are white. The recording industries in North America and Europe haven't always given people equal opportunities to succeed.

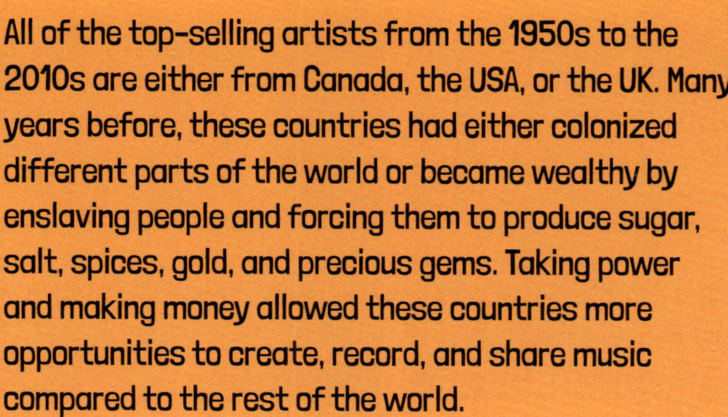

All of the top-selling artists from the 1950s to the 2010s are either from Canada, the USA, or the UK. Many years before, these countries had either colonized different parts of the world or became wealthy by enslaving people and forcing them to produce sugar, salt, spices, gold, and precious gems. Taking power and making money allowed these countries more opportunities to create, record, and share music compared to the rest of the world.

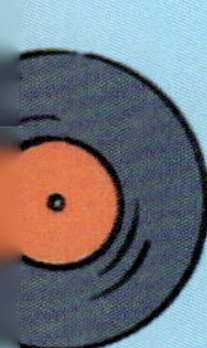

Because of colonization, English is the world's most spoken language. But there has always been a lot of amazing music being made in other languages. People such as Xiao Zhan from China and Helene Fischer from Germany have sold millions of records, but often they are not as internationally recognized as people who sing in English.

SOME BEST-SELLING ARTISTS

ABBA	Sweden
THE BEATLES	UK
BEYONCE	USA
HELENE FISCHER	Germany
NAZIA AND ZOHEB	Pakistan
RAIHAN	Malaysia
RIHANNA	Barbados
TAYLOR SWIFT	USA
THONGCHAI MCINTYRE	Thailand

In the next chapter, we'll take a look at some of the instruments from around the world that make this **awesome music possible.**

Chapter 5

Instruments

Musical instruments come in all shapes and sizes, and people use them to express their thoughts and feelings, and communicate ideas in many different ways. While we can't look at every instrument ever invented, here are a few that are historically important or are used in a lot of music today.

Old instruments

Archaeologists have found fragments of bone that may have been ancient musical instruments.

The Hohle Fels flute is about 40,000 years old! It was discovered in Germany and is made out of animal bone.

pūrerehua

Hohle Fels flute

A pūrerehua is a Māori instrument, dating back thousands of years. It is usually made from stone, wood, or bone.

The Bull Headed Lyre of Ur was found in Mesopotamia. It is about 4,000 years old and is one of the oldest string instruments ever discovered.

Many more instruments have been found or created in the last 2,000 years, and they are usually put into four categories: woodwind, percussion, brass, and strings. These categories exclude all the electronic instruments we use today.

The Hornbostel-Sachs system of classifying instruments was designed by Erich Hornbostel and Curt Sachs in 1914, and is very complicated (with over 300 categories!). In 2020, the music educator Steve Giddings simplified their system. His approach is a great way of understanding how instruments are related to each other, so it's the one we'll use here . . .

Wind instruments (Aerophones)

These instruments include anything that you blow into, no matter what they are made from or how you blow into them. Wood, metal, and clay have all been used to create wind instruments.

Woodwind instruments like saxophones and clarinets (both from Western Europe), use a single reed made from wood that vibrates to create sound when it's blown.

Others, like duduks (Armenia) and oboes (Western Europe), use two reeds, and are called double reed instruments.

clarinet

duduk

Other wind instruments do not use reeds, and many brass instruments require the player's lips to vibrate to produce sound. These include trumpets (the oldest is over 3,000 years old and was found in Egypt) and trombones, which were invented in Western Europe.

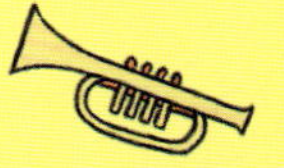

Another example is the saxophone. The Belgian instrument maker Adolphe Sax invented the saxophone in the 1840s. Although many people think of saxophones as jazz instruments, they were first used in classical music.

As jazz evolved and became more popular in the USA, saxophonists such as Lester Young and Coleman Hawkins became well-respected musicians. In the 1940s, Charlie Parker took the instrument to new levels, by the speed of his playing and his note choices, with a style of jazz called **bebop.**

saxophone

CHARLIE PARKER

One of the most influential saxophone players of all time. He was nicknamed "Bird."

Percussion (Idiophones)

These are instruments you hit, tap, or scrape to produce sound.

Drums are made by stretching a membrane made of plastic, animal skin, or other material over a structure. The mridangam (South Asia) and the djembe (West Africa) both make sound when their membrane is hit, scratched, or flicked.

djembe

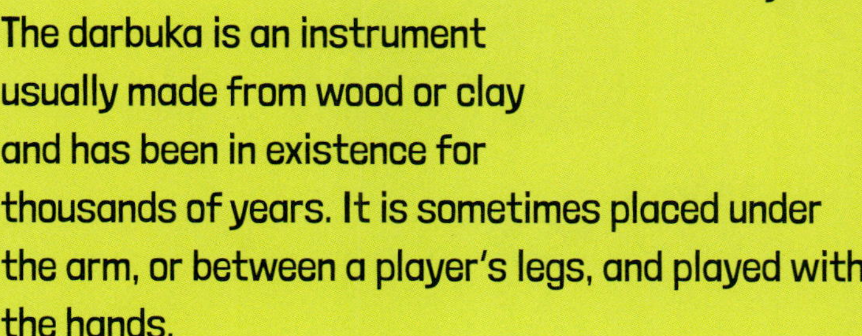

The darbuka is an instrument usually made from wood or clay and has been in existence for thousands of years. It is sometimes placed under the arm, or between a player's legs, and played with the hands.

Xylophones, gongs (from Southeast Asia) and steelpans (from Trinidad and Tobago) don't have membranes on them, but they make sound when they are either hit with mallets or struck against each other like cymbals.

There are other percussion instruments that make sounds when they are plucked or flicked, like mbira, jaw harps, and music boxes.

The mbira (or kalimba) consists of a wooden board and metal prongs that are played with the thumbs —that is why it is sometimes called a "thumb piano." It originates from the area now known as Zimbabwe and is estimated to have been invented over 2,000 years ago.

Strings

Violins, erhus, tanburs, and koras are all instruments that make a sound when a musician vibrates their strings in some way. These strings are bowed, plucked, picked, or even slapped. These instruments often have large ranges too.

Speak like a Musician

RANGE

The range is the distance between the lowest and the highest notes a person can sing, or an instrument can play.

The sitar is one of the most widely recognized instruments in southern Asia. It is often featured in Hindustani classical music and originated in the seventh century in India. It is often made with between eighteen and twenty-one strings.
The **virtuosic** (excellent) sitar player Ravi Shankar is credited with helping make the sitar more recognized around the world in the twentieth century.

MUSIC HERO

RAVI SHANKAR

Sitar player who released more than seventy albums and performed around the world for over fifty years.

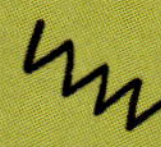

The kora instrument originates from West Africa and is usually made from a dried calabash, a type of fruit. Over the past 900 years it has been played in many different styles, including traditional styles from Mali and the Gambia as well as jazz. It has twenty-two strings, which musicians pluck with their fingers (that's a lot of fingers!).

Speak like a Musician

STRING TECHNIQUES

There are special words in Italian that string players use to describe different techniques. Some of these include acro (with the bow), pizzicato (to pluck), and tremolo (repeatedly playing one note quickly).

The kora was traditionally only played by men, but players like Toumani Diabaté from Mali, and the British Gambian musician Sona Jobarteh, have created music in many styles, which has helped to make the kora more popular. Toumani Diabaté comes from a family of griots, and his cousin, Sona Jobarteh has performed worldwide with orchestras and also written music for a film.

MUSIC HERO

SONA JOBARTEH

Virtuosic professional kora player, and the first female in a profession reserved for men for hundreds of years in her family history.

Electronic

Electricity has been used more and more to make music over the last 100 years. There are instruments that rely solely on electricity, such as synthesizers and theremins, and other instruments, like electric guitars and bass guitars, that make sounds by themselves but need electricity to amplify that sound. Also, musicians often use different effect pedals to layer sounds or add cool or unusual effects.

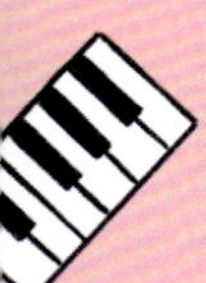

synthesizer

The **synthesizer** (or synth) is perhaps the most widely used electronic instrument. Synthesizers come in all shapes and sizes and can produce many interesting and unusual sounds. Musicians such as Keith Emerson and Stevie Wonder helped make them popular in the 1970s.

Many of Stevie Wonder's hit songs, such as "Superstition," used a synthesizer called **TONTO** (The Original New Timbral Orchestra). At over twenty feet wide and six feet high, it is approximately the same size as four bathtubs wide and one fridge high!

MUSIC HERO

STEVIE WONDER

Multi-instrumentalist and singer who is famous for his use of synthesizers and his unique voice. Blind from shortly after birth, he was a skilled musician by the age of eight.

Nowadays you will hear a synthesizer on almost every single pop record you can get your hands on . . . or ears on?

The next instrument is probably the **most important of all . . .**

Voice

The first music we made as humans was with our voices! As humans evolved words and language, we developed different ways of **expressing our emotions** through the sounds we made. Even before people used words, they probably made sounds with their mouths and voices, perhaps copying the sounds they heard in nature.

For many people, the voice is our first instrument, and the one that connects us to others. It is the first instrument that many parents use to soothe babies, as well as the one often used to celebrate or mourn. Even today, the voice is the central feature for many styles including the **blues**, **opera**, and **gospel**. Singers, rather than instrumentalists, are the most well-known musicians in the world.

Lata Mangeshkar was an Indian singer who was so iconic that when she passed away in 2022, she was given a state funeral and mourned by millions around the world.

MUSIC HERO

LATA MANGESHKAR

One of the most recorded singers of all time. She sang in over 1,000 Bollywood movies.

In countries such as Mongolia, and regions such as southern Siberia and the Arctic, some communities practice throat singing. Using these ancient techniques, people have developed the ability to sing two or even three sounds at the same time.

It's not just about how someone sings—the lyrics of a song are extremely important too in helping us connect with each other.

Speak like a Musician

LYRICS

Lyrics are the words in a piece of music.

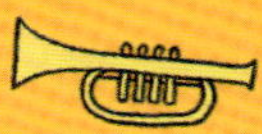

Beatboxing

Beatboxing evolved in North America in the late 1980s, as people including Doug E. Fresh provided beats using their voices for rappers to rap over. At first beatboxing backed rappers and singers, but it has now become an art form in itself, and there are competitions held all over the world. American Kaila Mullady is a Beatbox Battle World Champion, having won the Individual Female category in 2015 and 2018. To do your own beatboxing, say **"boots and cats and boots and cats"** over and over . . .

People in different places around the world used all of these instruments to create music that spoke to them and their communities. In the next chapter, we'll explore some of these styles of music.

folk
samba
funk
reggae
rock
pop
jazz
blues
bambuca
hip-hop
soul
afrobeats

Chapter 6

Styles of Music

There are many different styles of music that have developed independently around the world.

As cultures collided with each other, more and more new styles evolved. We can't talk about all the different styles of music, but here are a few that have had a big impact.

From West Africa to the Americas

The Transatlantic Slave Trade lasted for over 400 years from the sixteenth to the nineteenth century. During this time, it is estimated that up to twelve million West Africans were enslaved by various Western European nations and taken to South America, the Caribbean, and North America.

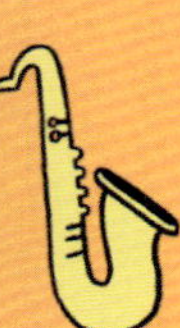

Enslaved West Africans had musical traditions that were **thousands of years old,** but many were banned from playing their music, owning instruments, or even being allowed to read or write.

But this didn't stop them from creating music. The need for people to express sadness, joy, and hope over generations of enslavement produced different styles of music that are still popular today.

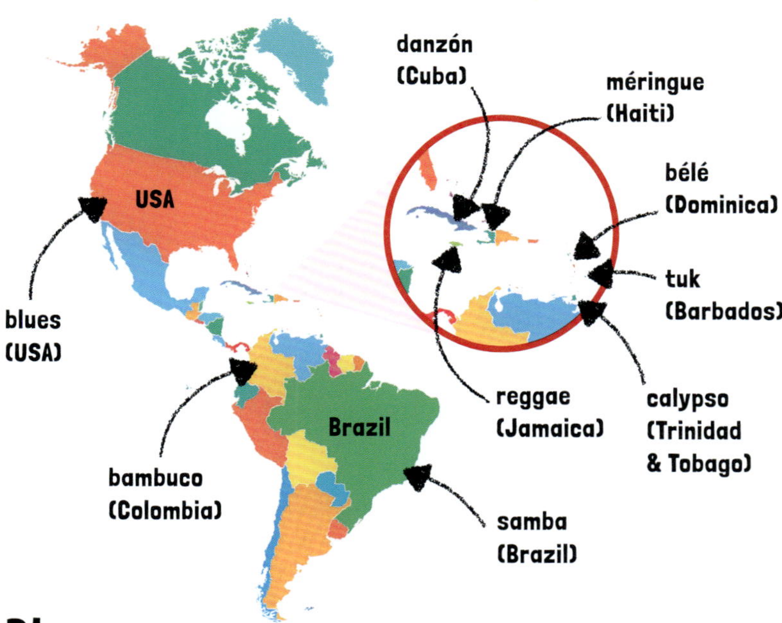

Blues

The blues was developed in the American Deep South in the mid-nineteenth century by the descendants of enslaved Africans. The ways chords are used, and melodic techniques such as call and response, are some of the main features of the style. Guitars, banjos, percussion, and vocals were some of the instruments people used to express themselves. The blues became the foundation for jazz and a lot of modern **pop music**.

We have people such as the guitarist Robert Johnson and vocalist Ma Rainey to thank for popularizing it!

MUSIC HERO

MA RAINEY

Known as "the Mother of the Blues," she was pioneering in more ways than one, with some of her songs referencing her bisexuality.

Jazz

Jazz (originally written "jass") evolved in the USA in the late nineteenth century. Black musicians were at the forefront of this style. Jazz bands (like quartets) often consist of piano, bass, and drums (called the rhythm section), and one instrument that plays the melody (trumpet or saxophone). Big bands can also feature a large horn section, guitar, or **vibraphone**.

Speak like a Musician

HORN SECTION

A collection of trumpets, trombones, and saxophones playing together is called a horn section.

One of the main features of jazz is improvisation. The trumpeter Louis Armstrong improvised using his voice and nonsense syllables in a technique called scatting in the 1920s.

The way he scatted and improvised on his trumpet was unique, and he is considered one of the most influential people in American music history (if not the most!).

Speak like a Musician

IMPROVISATION

Improvisation is when musicians spontaneously create music on an instrument, including their voice.

MUSIC HERO

LOUIS ARMSTRONG

American trumpeter and vocalist, and one of the most important figures in jazz history.

Jazz produced many incredible singers such as Ella Fitzgerald, whose scatting was so good that many musicians looked up to and copied her style. Jazz evolved through the twentieth century with musicians such as

Miles Davis, who constantly changed, blended styles, and used electronic instruments in a fifty-year career!

Jazz has been fused with styles from around the world by people such as Yazz Ahmed, a British Bahrani trumpet player who blends jazz with Arabic influences. Chucho Valdés is a pianist who uses Afro-Cuban elements in his music, while Esperanza Spalding, an American bass player and singer, is known for her compositions and ability to sing in different languages and play the bass at the same time.

MUSIC HERO

ESPERANZA SPALDING

Award-winning singer, bass player, and composer.

Afrobeat/Afrobeats

Afrobeat is a style of music from West Africa combining a few different styles from the region to create upbeat and lively music, popularized by the Nigerian multi-instrumentalist Fela Kuti. He was also a politician who used his music to talk about politics. In the last twenty years, a new style called **afrobeats** has combined hip-hop, pop, and Afrobeat to give us artists like WizKid and Burna Boy.

MUSIC HERO

FELA KUTI

Multi-instrumentalist and politician from Nigeria.

Indian classical music

Classical music in India can generally be split into two styles: Hindustani and **Carnatic**. Hindustani music comes from northern regions of India, while Carnatic comes from the south. There are many differences between the styles, including the musical **ornamentation** used, and the different languages that the music is sung in. Generally, Carnatic music focuses more on compositions and lyrics, while Hindustani music emphasizes understanding of **rāga** and improvisation.

Hindustani instruments include the sitar, sarangi, and tabla.

sitar

Carnatic instruments include the violin, ghatam, and mridangam.

mridangam

Pop

Pop music is a style of music that is designed to appeal to as many people as possible. It often features drums, bass, synthesizers, and vocals. Pop artists who sing in English, like Beyoncé, are some of the world's most famous people.

Different countries have their own versions of pop music, from C-pop in China to K-pop in Korea. The Korean band BTS is currently the most popular pop band in the world.

MUSIC HERO

BEYONCÉ

One of the world's biggest superstars. She has sold millions of albums, won thirty-two Grammy Awards, and acted in, and written music for, films including *Dreamgirls* and *The Lion King*.

Hip-hop

Rapping combined with looped beats is the foundation of hip-hop. Many agree that this style of music was born at a birthday party in New York on August 11, 1973. Since then, hip-hop has become one of the most popular musical genres on Earth, with people rapping in different languages and producers blending other styles of music with it. Since the 1970s, hip-hop has evolved into many different forms, including grime, crunk, conscious, and trap.

You don't need to play an instrument to take part. People rap about many things, including their personal experiences, issues in society, and good times with friends. New York rapper Queen Latifah used hip-hop to talk about women's rights in the early 1990s, and many other rappers, like Common, speak about positive thinking and believing in yourself.

The superstar rapper Jay-Z has had a string of hits since the mid-1990s. He has collaborated with many musicians, including his wife, Beyoncé, and has won many awards in his twenty-five year career.

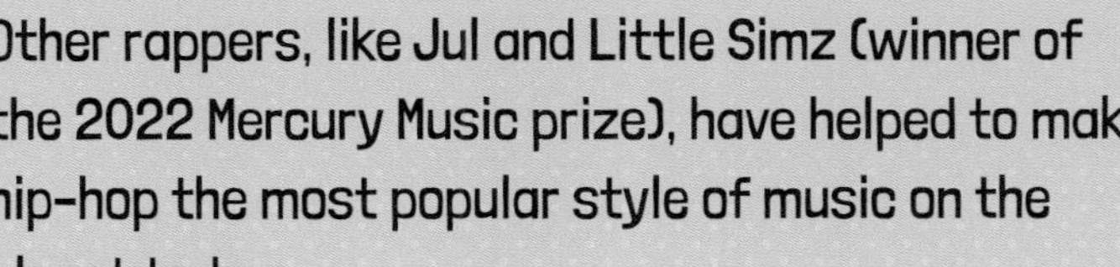

Other rappers, like Jul and Little Simz (winner of the 2022 Mercury Music prize), have helped to make hip-hop the most popular style of music on the planet today.

Hip-hop has traditionally centered around DJs and emcees, but artists will often perform with live bands, and occasionally with horn sections and stringed instruments.

Reggae

Reggae music comes from the Caribbean island of Jamaica, and was developed in the 1960s.

Its heavily syncopated rhythms and relaxed tempo make the style one of the most recognizable in the world. Organs, guitars, bass guitars, and drums are commonly used in reggae, often with vocals as the focus of the song.

Bob Marley and his band The Wailers are credited with bringing reggae and Jamaican culture to audiences worldwide with songs like "Three Little Birds" and "No Woman No Cry."

The music often contained inspirational lyrics that are **still relevent today** and commented on global events in the 1960s and 1970s, such as various African countries gaining independence.

As reggae spread around the world, it helped to influence the creation of other styles including hip-hop. Artists such as Koffee continue to make reggae music, and she became the first woman to win a Grammy for best reggae album in 2020.

MUSIC HERO

BOB MARLEY

Jamaican singer who is probably the most famous reggae musician ever!

Rock

Rock developed in the USA in the late 1940s and, like many other styles, has changed a lot over the years. Music by bands such as The Beatles and the Ronettes have their roots in rock and roll, and have inspired artists throughout the last seventy years, including Tina Turner and David Bowie.

David Bowie influenced many musicians all over world for over fifty years and constantly changed his style of music to reach new audiences.

Rock is known for heavy use of guitars, guitar solos, and heavy drum patterns. Sometimes it can sound "angry" and has been used in protest songs. The style has evolved into many different directions including heavy metal, punk rock, and glam rock.

MUSIC HERO

DAVID BOWIE

British musician and songwriter who sold over 100 million records worldwide.

Western European classical

The history of this music, up until the twentieth century, can be split into five broad styles from different time periods.

Medieval
about 500–1400

Renaissance
about 1400–1600

Baroque
about 1600–1750

Classical
about 1750–1820

Romantic
about 1820–1920

The period from 1750–1820 produced some of the world's most iconic music, which some people feel is the best music Western Europeans have ever created. These pieces often featured powerful melodies and themes, shared among different instruments with dramatic loud and soft sections. As composers created longer pieces of music, they began to use more instruments and started to expand the European classical orchestra into roughly what we see today.

EXAMPLE LAYOUT OF THE INSTRUMENTS FOR A MODERN ORCHESTRA

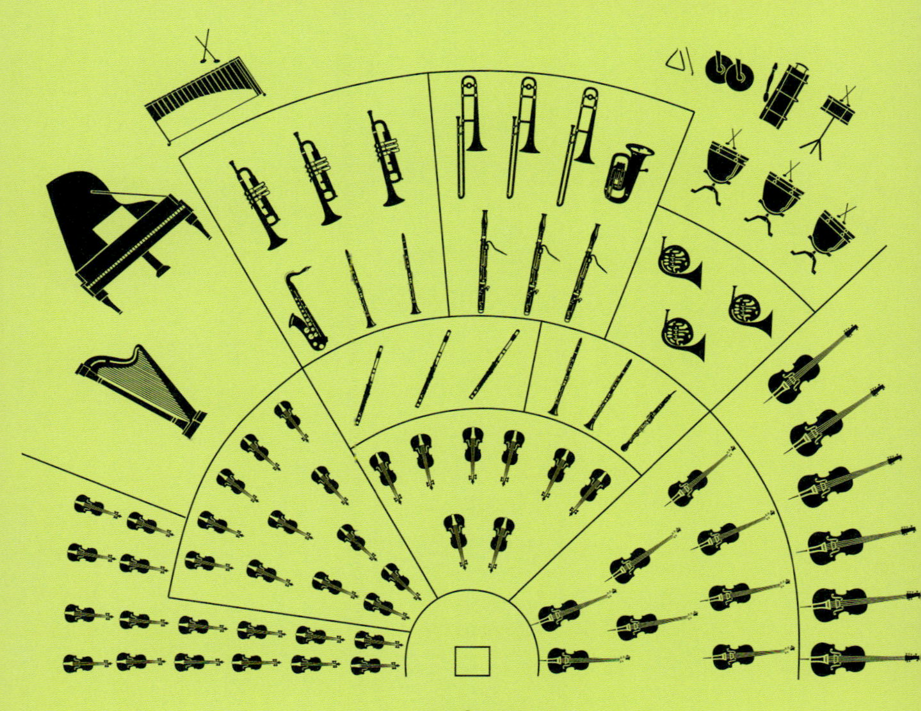

conductor

Unfortunately, women, trans, and non-binary people have rarely been treated as equal to men throughout European music history, but there have always been a few women recognized as incredible musicians and composers through history. Even way back in the twelfth century, Hildegard von Bingen was acknowledged as a phenomenal composer of beautiful **monophonic** music.

Speak like a Musician

MONOPHONIC

Monophonic music is music that is made up of a simple melody without accompaniment.

Composers such as Joseph Haydn and Ludwig van Beethoven were making music in the 1700s and 1800s, as well as the Austrian composer and child prodigy Wolfgang Amadeus Mozart. He started writing music when he was about five years old, and in his short life (he died when he was thirty-five), he wrote over 800 pieces, including forty-one symphonies.

MUSIC HERO

WOLFGANG AMADEUS MOZART

One of the most influential European composers of the classical era.

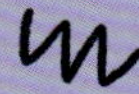

At this time, classical music centered around the areas now known as Germany and Austria. In the twentieth century, more people from outside of Europe started to create music in similar styles.

Florence Price was an American musician who wrote in this style. In 1993 she became the first Black American woman to have a symphony played by a major American orchestra.

MUSIC HERO

FLORENCE PRICE

One of the first internationally recognized Black women composers in European classical music.

In the next chapter, we'll take a look at how people have used these and other styles to fight wars, protest, **and make people's lives better . . .**

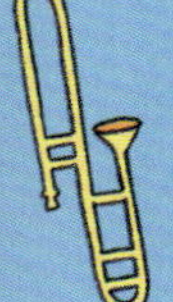

Chapter 7

Music as a Force for Change

Outside of entertainment and expressing emotions, music has been used throughout history to help make important changes in local communities, countries, and globally.

Music was used in war to help organize troops and frighten enemies. Marching bands originated in the Ottoman Empire in the thirteenth century, and fife and drum bands have been used from Scotland to Barbados. These bands still exist today, but might be used to entertain tourists or help celebrate special days.

Sikh military band

African American songs of freedom

WORK SONGS

Work songs were sung by enslaved West Africans and African Americans while doing manual labor in the eighteenth and nineteenth centuries. These songs might contain information about the kind of work being done, or about how they were feeling.

The work song "Old Cotton, Old Corn" is about the work enslaved women were forced to do:

OLD COTTON, OLD CORN

Old cotton, old corn, see you every morn
Old cotton, old corn, see you since I was born
Old cotton, old corn, hoe you till dawn
Old cotton, old corn, what for you born?

SPIRITUALS

Taking their inspiration from the Bible, spirituals were sometimes sung by enslaved people to help other enslaved people escape. Singing the song "Steal Away," for example, may have alerted other enslaved people that someone was planning to escape soon, and "Wade in the Water" may have been sung to tell people to walk in a river or stream to reduce the chance of dogs picking up their scent as they escaped to freedom.

These songs could be **vital for survival**, as many enslaved people were forbidden from learning how to read or write.

Music against racism

After slavery was abolished in America, Black Americans were still victims of racism and segregation.

In the twentieth century, especially after recorded music became more accessible, more and more musicians started to use music as a way to express their feelings about issues in society. Not everyone in North America could read well, or had access to printed media. This music could also encourage people to take action, remind them that they weren't alone in feeling angry, hurt, or frustrated, and tell others about what was happening in the world.

One of the most famous **protest** songs is "Strange Fruit." It was written by a Jewish composer called Abel Meeropol and recorded by American jazz vocalist Billie Holiday in 1937. The song describes how Black Americans were murdered by racist white people and their bodies hung from trees, almost resembling fruit swaying in the wind. She performed this song in front of white audiences, which was incredibly brave, and Holiday's personal connection with the song, because she was descended from enslaved people, means that it's still powerful and haunting.

MUSIC HERO

BILLIE HOLIDAY

Influential jazz singer known for her ability to improvise.

The US civil rights movement in the 1950s and 1960s was Black Americans' struggle to end segregation, discrimination, and racism.

Musicians used jazz, soul, and other styles to create music that talked about these issues. The pianist and singer Nina Simone dedicated most of her professional career to writing music about how Black Americans were being treated.

Concerts such as the Harlem Cultural Festival in 1969 brought thousands of people together to protest against violence and discrimination. Musicians including Stevie Wonder and the soul and funk band Sly and the Family Stone performed to show support for the movement.

Indigenous Americans

With colonization, Western Europeans took land from the people who had lived there for thousands of years.

Many Indigenous people were slaughtered by the colonizers and their music, dancing, and languages were banned at different places and times.

Ever since then, Indigenous peoples have been fighting for ownership of land, representation, and equal rights by campaigning, protesting, and, of course, through music.

Buffy Sainte-Marie is a musician of the Cree Nation who has dedicated her musical career to speaking about issues that Indigenous peoples face. Her song called "Now that the Buffalo's Gone" was written in 1964 about land being taken from Indigenous peoples. It's a simple song, but Sainte-Marie's voice is full of emotion:

NOW THAT THE BUFFALO'S GONE

Has a change come about my dear man?

Or are you still taking our lands

A treaty forever your senators sign

They do dear lady, they do dear man

And the treaties are broken again and again

And what will you do for these ones?

Australia

Aboriginal and Torres Strait Islander peoples are the original inhabitants of Australia. The colonization of Australia erased many traditional ways of life in many Aboriginal communities. In 2018, the musician Mo'Ju wrote a song called "Native Tongue," which spoke about her search for identity and the racial tensions that still exist in her country.

South Africa

South African apartheid was a racist system that aimed to keep Black South Africans away from white South Africans. This system was in place for almost fifty years, and a lot of music was written in protest, including by jazz musician Hugh Masekela.

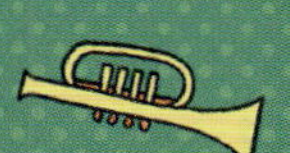

He wrote a powerful song called "Soweto Blues" after hundreds of people, including children, were murdered by the police in Soweto, South Africa, in 1976. And in 1987, his song "Bring Him Back Home" protested against apartheid and the imprisonment of the future South African President, Nelson Mandela.

MUSIC HERO

HUGH MASEKELA

Influential South African jazz musician who used his music to protest against racism.

WE WANT JUSTICE!

ACT NOW!

Black Lives Matter

In June 2020 the very public murder of George Floyd brought to a head a spate of Black Americans' deaths caused by police officers and reignited public interest in the Black Lives Matter movement.

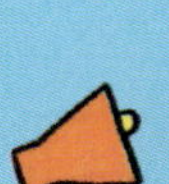

Musicians from all over the world made music in response, but it was a 2013 song by American musician Janelle Monáe that was played again and again. The lyrics of "Hell You Talmbout" encouraged people to say the names of the numerous Black people who have died at the hands of the police. The British rapper Jords used Black Lives Matter chants from a march as part of the beat for his song "Black and Ready."

Israeli-Palestinian conflict

Since 1948, there have been violent and ongoing conflicts between Israeli and Palestinian people, and many have written music about the effects it has had on their communities, and the need for peace. Reem Kelani is a musician of Palestinian descent whose music explores how the conflict has affected the region. She stands together with many artists as they call for peace.

MARCH FOR PEACE

Women's rights

Women around the world have campaigned and protested for the right to vote, abortion rights, education, and other issues for over 100 years, often using music in the process. "Eliza Jane" was written back in 1895 about a woman riding a bicycle.

In Western Europe at that time, women wearing trousers was shocking to some people, but the freedom was liberating.

ELIZA JANE

No more do skirts enfold her,
tho' much her papa grieves,

But baggy trousers hold her in
their big pneumatic sleeves;

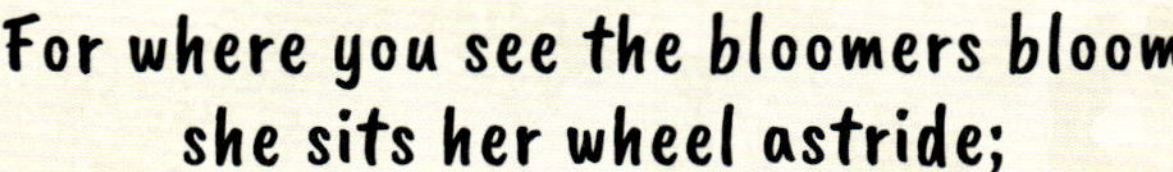

For where you see the bloomers bloom
she sits her wheel astride;

She makes a sight would stop a fight
as in the park she rides.

Continuing the tradition nearly seventy years later, seventeen-year-old Lesley Gore recorded a song called "You Don't Own Me" in 1963 which spoke about how she should be able to **live her life** without anyone telling her what to do.

In Mauritania, the vocalist Malouma has been making music to support the rights of women, especially for those who identify as Muslim. Her music has empowered many, but has **angered** various governments as some of her music speaks about the treatment of women in society and freedom of speech.

MUSIC HERO

MALOUMA

Mauritanian vocalist who has been outspoken in support of Muslim women everywhere.

LGBTQIA+

In the last ten years, more and more people have made music about LGBTQIA+ (Lesbian, Gay, Bisexual, Transgender, Queer or Questioning, Intersex and Allies, Aromantic or Agender +) rights. It isn't always easy for musicians to be open about their gender or sexuality, but music has helped others to feel more confident and see that they are not alone in how they feel.

Superstars like the pianist and songwriter Elton John are open about their sexuality now, but it wasn't as easy to be so free and open when he was starting out in the 1970s.

Elton John

In 1980, Diana Ross released "I'm Coming Out" whose lyrics spoke about letting the world know who you are and being fearless in the process. These themes led to it being adopted as an anthem for the LGBTQIA+ communities.

More recently, the musician Bashar Murad has spoken about how music helped him growing up in East Jerusalem and the USA as a queer man. And in 2022, Sam Smith wrote a song about how they feel about themselves, called "Love Me More," expressing that they have felt hatred toward themselves in the past, and that they are finally accepting who they are.

In the next chapter we'll look at how music works in the background. One of the cool things about music is that it doesn't always tell you what to think or what to feel, but is often affecting us **even if we don't realize it . . .**

Chapter 8

Music in the Background

When you think of music, you probably think about concerts, records, or even dance moves. However, you might be surprised by how much music is all around us every day and how it affects us.

The sound of shopping

Have you ever thought about **why** music is played in supermarkets or other stores?

Scientists and psychologists have conducted experiments over the past fifty years to try and understand if the music you hear when shopping has an effect on how you shop—and it does! A study found that playing slow music caused customers to spend much more time in a store. Other studies have shown that people generally spend more time in stores that play soft music than those that play loud music.

A different study showed that if people heard music they knew in a store, they spent more time in the store than if unfamiliar music was playing.

This shows how "in tune" people are with music and sound. Even if people are not paying attention to melodies or chords, music has the ability to affect our **subconcious** and change our behavior. The more familiar and comfortable we are in an environment, the more time we'll spend there. Large businesses can use this knowledge to their advantage.

Video games

Playing your favorite video game without music might be **a very different experience!** Since video games developed the ability to include music in the late 1970s and early 1980s, people have specialized in creating video game music.

In the 1980s, video games couldn't process more than two or three simple electronic sounds at a time, but those sounds still created a different playing experience.

Koji Kondo is best known for writing the music for the original Super Mario Bros. The music changed if Mario was in a dungeon or underwater, and sped up when time was running out to complete a level! This added extra tension and excitement and is one of the reasons why the game is still so iconic thirty years later.

Now consoles have become more powerful, some games even use popular rock, hip-hop, or pop music, and allow players to choose whatever music they want to listen to.

MUSIC HERO

KOJI KONDO

Japanese composer who created music for an Italian plumber called Super Mario in the famous video game.

Advertisements

You'll rarely see an ad on TV without any music! That's because research has shown that music helps people to remember information more easily—many companies create catchy jingles with a simple slogan or with the name of their company. In 2003, the vocalist Justin Timberlake recorded a song called "I'm Lovin' It" which has been the McDonald's jingle ever since. These days, millions of people only need to hear these five notes to be reminded of McDonald's—whether they want to or not!

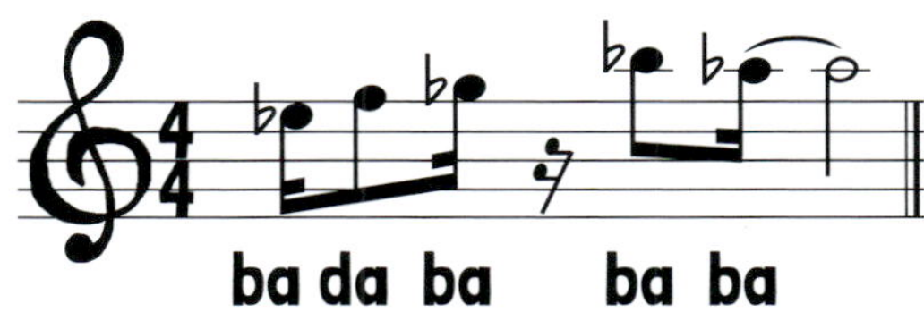

Film

Music composed especially for a film helps to reveal characters' emotions, increase drama, or relieve tension. Fast music during a car chase can make it more dramatic, while a slow violin during a sad moment may tug on your heartstrings a little bit more.

The first films had no sound in them, and any speech would appear in writing on the screen. Sometimes these silent movies were shown with a pianist or small ensemble playing live music to accompany the film.

In the USA, *The Jazz Singer* was the first feature length movie to have synchronized sound in 1927. The phenomenon spread around the world to countries such as Germany and China in the early 1930s.

Filmmakers started to realize the importance of having music in their films and began to pay people to create unique music for them, rather than using existing music written by famous composers.

Composers including John Williams are known for the iconic film scores they have written in the Hollywood (USA) film industry.

Williams wrote the music for the first three *Harry Potter* movies, and perhaps most famously, for *Star Wars*.

Film music industries around the world have been dominated by men, but in the last twenty-five years more women have become well known for their film music. The Turkish American composer Pinar Toprak wrote the music for *Captain Marvel* in 2019, has written for TV, and even for the video game Fortnite!

MUSIC HERO

PINAR TOPRAK

One of a few women of color who have created music for blockbuster Hollywood films.

Instruments of the Western European orchestra and synthesizers are commonly used, but in film industries such as Nollywood (Nigeria) and Bollywood (India), local instruments and styles are also used. R.D. Burman was an Indian film composer who used funk, rock, and Hindustani musical influences in famous movies like *Sanam Teri Kasam* and *Yaadon Ki Baaraat.*

MUSIC HERO

R.D. BURMAN

Indian composer and musical director of more than 300 films in Bollywood.

Nowadays, film scores and original songs are often just as important as the films themselves.

Songwriters such as Robert Lopez and Kristen Anderson-Lopez have written some of the most well-known music of the last ten years for films such as *Frozen* and *Frozen II.*

Many songs written by Lin-Manuel Miranda have become popular all over the world—"We Don't Talk About Bruno" from *Encanto* (2021) has become one of Disney's most successful songs and reached number one in the USA, UK, and Ireland.

MUSIC HERO

LIN-MANUEL MIRANDA

Award-winning composer who has written an amazing amount of catchy music for films including *Moana*.

We've looked at a lot of music that we already know, but what about the future?

Let's look into our musical crystal ball and imagine.

Chapter 9

Imagining the Future

As we've seen throughout this book, technology has made listening to and making music so much easier over the last 100 years, from records to streaming, from the tanbur to the electric guitar. What might music be like in another 100 years?

Virtual Reality (VR) and Augmented Reality (AR) might change the way we experience live music in the future. We might be able to sit at home with a headset on and watch a live concert along with millions of other people from around the world. While we are watching the concert, we might be able to sit, talk, or even dance with someone far away!

VR also means we could be playing in bands with people from around the world, maybe even using translation programs in real time to help us communicate. Concerts and collaborations like this could mean fewer people traveling, which would be better for the environment.

As good as this might sound, perhaps we may lose some of the **human connections** we make when we create and listen to music with people in person, and the experience of feeling the music in our bodies.

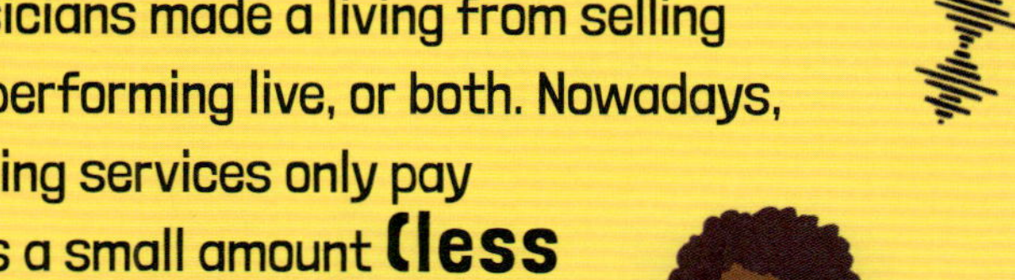

Before we were able to download and stream music, many musicians made a living from selling records or performing live, or both. Nowadays, streaming services only pay artists a small amount **(less than one cent per stream!)**, so other ways of making a living through music will have to be found.

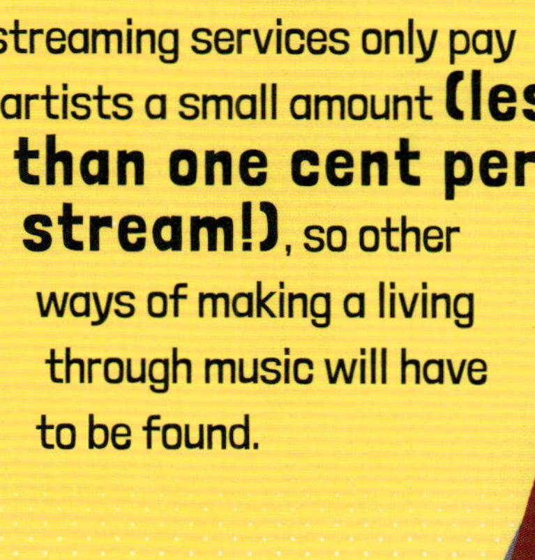

Now that social media platforms allow artists to communicate directly with fans, we could see more artists using virtual reality to give concerts and connect with their audience.

Artificial Intelligence (AI) may understand us so well that streaming services will be able to play the exact song we need to lift our mood, or to keep us focused or excited. On the other hand, if you've ever had a song stuck in your head but you can't remember what it's called, technology could allow us to hum or sing a song (no matter how badly we do it) and find it instantly!

Better technology could help disabled people express themselves through music in more ways. Devices like MiMU gloves, which connect with music software, already help people with limited mobility to create music using simple gestures.

With these MiMU gloves I have music at my fingertips!

MiMU gloves

There are also devices that allow people to play instruments like saxophones and trumpets with one hand, and instruments that can be controlled with the breath or eye movements.

How amazing would it be if technology allowed humans to control, play, and create instruments using only their minds?

Think how creative we could be!

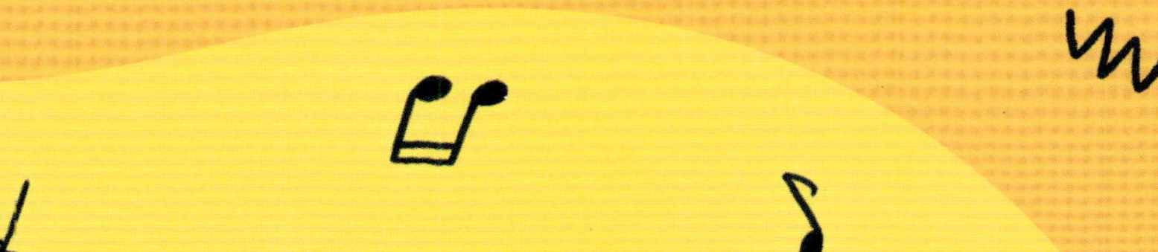

No matter what happens, because music is an important part of who we are, it will always be part of our world! It's going to be fascinating to be listening to, making, and **expressing ourselves through music in the future!**

Glossary

acro played with the bow (on a string instrument)

Afrobeat style of music that evolved in West Africa in the 1960s

amplify make a sound stronger, usually by making it louder

arpeggio the notes of a chord played in ascending or descending order

audio another word for sound

Baroque period of music from Western Europe in the 1600s to 1750

beatboxing the art of making beats using vocal cords

bebop style of jazz that developed in the 1940s

blues style of music developed in the the USA's Deep South during the mid-nineteenth century

breaks the parts in a hip-hop track mainly featuring solo drums

Carnatic music style of classical music from the south of India

chords three or more notes played at the same time

cello large string instrument from Western Europe

colonization one nation or country taking political control over another, and taking the colonized country's resources and land

composer someone who creates music

decibels the units used when measuring the volume (loudness) of a sound

equal temperament the system that divides an octave into twelve equal parts

emcee person who raps along to music

funk style of music that evolved in the 1960s in the USA

gospel style of music created by Black Americans in the nineteenth century

Hindustani music style of classical music from the northern part of India

hip-hop a style of music originating in New York in the early 1970s

Indian classical music from India that can be split into two main styles—Hindustani or Carnatic

improvise spontaneously create music on an instrument, including the voice

jazz style of music developed by Black Americans in the late nineteenth century

klezmer style of music developed by Ashkenazi Jews from Eastern and Central Europe in the sixteenth century

maqām system of scales in Arabic music

melody usually the most recognizable part of a piece of music; there can also be many melodies within one piece

monophonic music that is made up of a single melody

Mesopotamia region in Asia where the world's first civilizations developed

multitrack recordings the technology that allowed musicians to record separately on the same track

octave distance between two notes, one of which vibrates at twice the frequency as another

opera style of music from Italy developed in the sixteenth century

ornamentation flourishes added to a melody that can increase expression and decoration

oud a fretless stringed instrument from seventh-century Persia

pitch how high or low a sound is

pizzicato the Italian word for the technique of plucking a stringed instrument

percussionist someone who plays percussion instruments

pop music short way of saying popular music, also means music created to appeal to as many people as possible

qanun a Middle Eastern stringed instrument with 72–81 strings

rāga complex blend between a scale and a melodic concept, used for composition and improvisation in South Asian classical music

rhythm repeated pattern of sound

rock style of music originating in the USA

scales ordered sets of notes

score in music, a written form of composition

symphony long composition, usually for a Western European-style orchestra

synthesizer electronic instrument that usually uses a keyboard

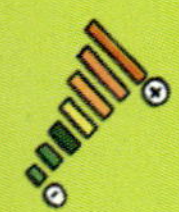

tempo how fast or slow a piece of music is

texture the number of different parts, or layers, in a piece of music—usually described as thick or thin

timbre the quality of sound that allows us to hear the difference between instruments or voices

tremolo repeatedly playing one note quickly on a string instrument

tuning systems that help us decide the different frequencies of notes

turntable piece of equipment DJs use to mix and "scratch" records

vibraphone percussion instrument made from metal bars and played with a mallet

virtuosic describes a musician who can play their instrument to an excellent, internationally recognized standard

vocal cords muscles in the throat that vibrate and produce the voice

wavelength the distance between individual vibrations of sound

Western European classical period of music from Western Europe from 1750 to 1830

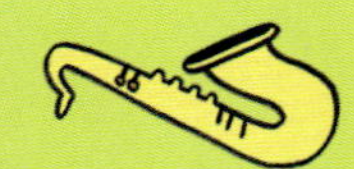

Index

Introducing the Music experts:

AUTHOR

PROFESSOR NATHAN HOLDER

Professor Nathan Holder is an accomplished musician and serves as International Chair of Music Education at the Royal Northern College of Music. As well as being a professor and music teacher, he is also an author and writes books for children about the history of music, where his purpose is to expand how we learn about music.

CONSULTANT

DR. DILJEET KAUR BHACHU

Dr. Diljeet Kaur Bhachu is an experienced musician, educator, and an avid activist for the decolonization of music. She sits as a consultant in arts and cultural sectors.

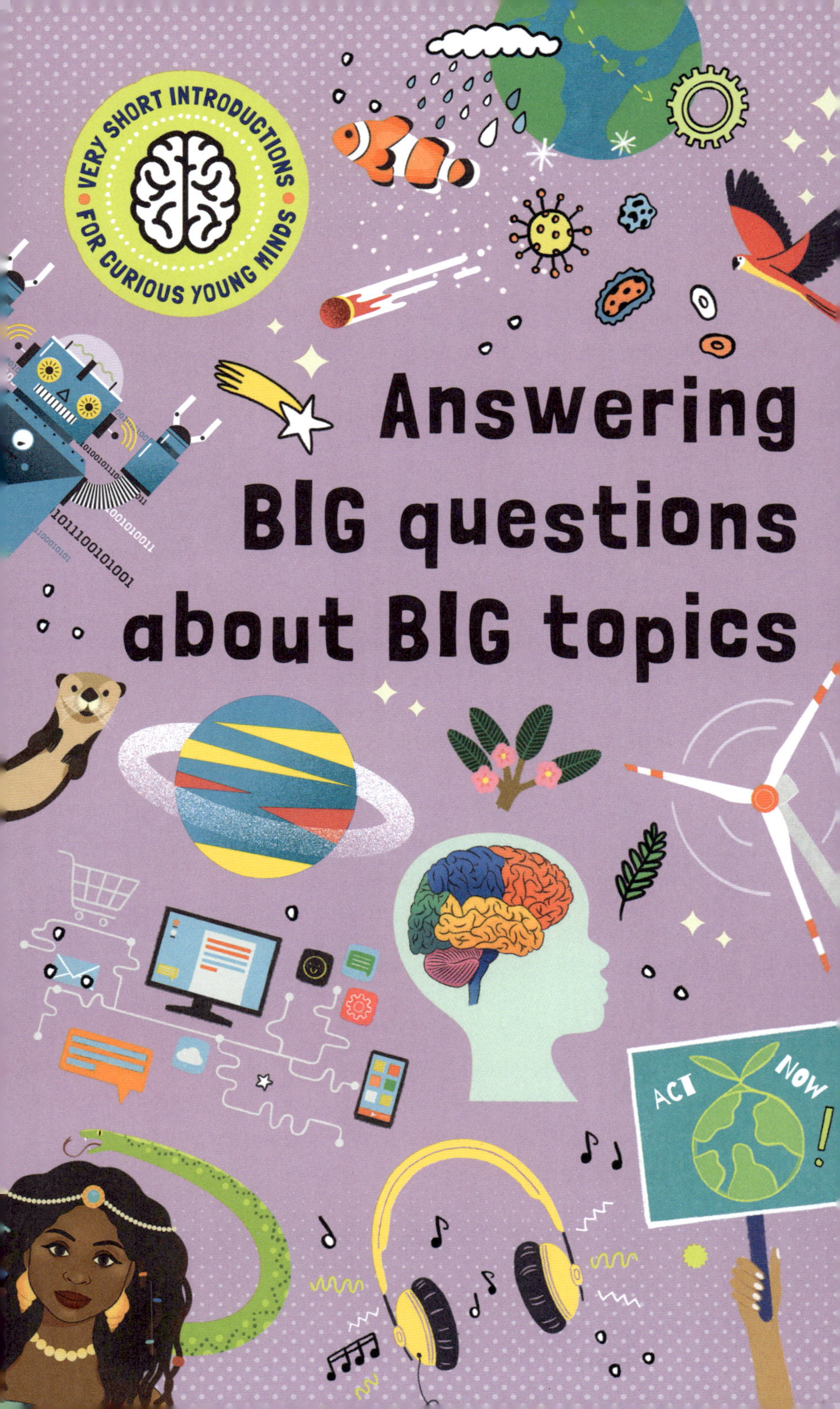
VERY SHORT INTRODUCTIONS
FOR CURIOUS YOUNG MINDS
Answering
BIG questions
about BIG topics
ACT
NOW
!